OTHER WORKS BY WILLIAM PITT ROOT

Poetry

    Reasons for Going It on Foot, 1981
    In the World's Common Grasses: Poems of a Son,
        Poems of a Father, 1981
    Striking the Dark Air for Music, 1973
    The Storm And Other Poems, 1969

Limited Editions

    The Unbroken Diamond: Nightletter to the
        Mujahadeen, 1983
    Fireclock, 1981
    Coot And Other Characters, 1977
    A Journey South, 1977
    7 Mendocino Songs, 1977
    Sheaf Poems: Collected Broadsides, 1977
    7 for a Magician, 1975

Translations

    Selected Odes of Pablo Neruda, 1984
    Ode to the Atom, Pablo Neruda, 1984
    The Invisible Man, Pablo Neruda, 1983

Films

    7 for a Magician, with Ray Rice, 1976
    Song of the Woman And the Butterflyman,
        with Ray Rice, 1975

Editor

    Timesoup: Poems & Art & Fiction by Young Alaskans,
        with Diane Katsiaficas, 1979
    Whataworld, Whataworld: Poems by Young
        People in Galveston, 1975
    Pipedream Press Pennypaper, with Guerny Norman,
        1970

INVISIBLE GUESTS
[an enlarged and revised edition of
Coot And Other Characters]

INVISIBLE GUESTS

William Pitt Root

Confluence Press, Inc.
at
Lewis-Clark State College
Lewiston, Idaho

ACKNOWLEDGMENTS

Most of these poems have appeared originally in periodicals, whose editors I wish to thank: *Arion's Dolphin, Atlantic Monthly, Beloit Poetry Journal, Berkshire Review, Blue Light, Blue Moon News, Catalyst* (Greensboro), *Cutbank, Counter/Measures, First Issue* (Brattleboro), *Florida Quarterly, Greensboro Review, Greenfield Review, Hudson Review, Jeopardy, Massachusetts Review, Mississippi Mud, The Nation, Poetry Now, Northwest Review, Sewanee Review, Southeast Arts Journal* (England), *Southwestern Review, Southern Poetry Review, Starroot, Vanderbilt Review, Writers Forum, Yarrow* and in the following anthologies: *Best Poems of 1974; A Decade of Poems from Southern Poetry Review; East Coast Poets; 80 for the 80's; Floating Gallery; The Generation of 2000: Thirty Contemporary Poets; The Point Riders Great Plains Anthology; Pushcart Prize Anthology; Rain in the Forest, Light in the Trees: A New Gathering of Northwest Poets; Since Feeling Is First; An Americas Anthology: A Geopoetics Landmark.* I also wish to thank the editors of *1980: A Calendar of Poetry And Photographs* and the *Mesilla Press Pamphlet Series.*

To Atheneum Publishers, thanks for permission to reprint here in a new context a number of poems from *The Storm And Other Poems* (1969), *Striking the Dark Air for Music* (1973), and *Reasons for Going It on Foot* (1981). My deep appreciation also is extended to Ray Rice, whose animated 16mm films based upon "Song of the Woman And the Butterflyman" and "7 for a Magician" have won honors at the International Poetry Film Festival and have shown me how extraordinarily gratifying collaboration can sometimes be. I wish to acknowledge my gratitude to Keith and Shirley Browning, who published most of these poems in the previous limited edition entitled *Coot And Other Characters* (1977). I want to acknowledge Rosa Guy's excellent *Children of Longing* as the source for "Why That Black Girl Picking Delta Cotton Will Be a Nurse."

Finally I would like to state my appreciation for a grant from the National Endowment of the Arts.

Copyright © 1984 by William Pitt Root
All Rights Reserved
Printed in the United States of America
ISBN 0-917652-28-2
Library of Congress Catalogue Card Number 83-073490
Cover by Arrow Graphics, Missoula, Montana

*This book is for everyone in whose life
I am a guest. It is especially for Pamela.*

CONTENTS

1. COOT

Meeting Coot, 15
Coot's Uses for His Shirts, 16
How Coot Got His Start, He Says, 17
How Words Taste And What Food Means, 18
Coot Tells It Like It Never Was, 19
Coot's Loneliness, Coot's Gold, 20
"Like Going Home", 21
Coot Takes a Look at *Cosmopolitan*, 22
How Coot Came to Speak Bear, 23
Coot And the Quiet, 25
Coot And the Golden Arches, 26
"Don't Matter to a Dog He Won't Reach China", 27
Coot And the Sperm Bank, 28
Coot And the Big Time, 29
Coot's Re-entry, 31
Coot's Lode, 32

2. "THESE ARE THE CHILDREN"

"By Their Own Truthful Masters", 35
Burning, 39
Curse of a Quiet Citizen, 41
Estrangements, 43
Death of a Family, 44
Ceremony, 45
Oldtimers, 48
The Last Days of a Retiring Executive, 50
I Go Out, 52
A Dream of Snow, 53
Year of the Monkey, 54
Whiteout, 57
"Do You Know the Country Around Here?", 58
Stoplight, 60
Truck Talking Late, 61
Voyeur, 64

Kansasman, 65
Words for the Dead, 67
For a Friend I've Lost Track of, 68
Idealist Out in the Weather, 69
Swansong, 70
Matron to Poet, 71
Galveston Seawall, 72
Cave-In, 74
Arc Welder Out in the Country, 78
Pox: A Prognosis, 80
"To Whom Shall I Speak And Give Warning?", 82

3. HOW THE PYGMY FOREST WORKS

Song of a Blind Traveller, 85
"And They Swam And They Swam", 86
Lord's Circus, 87
Why That Black Girl Picking Delta Cotton Will Be
   a Nurse, 89
Hermaphrodite's Ritual for Walking Past the Nine Windows
   In the Asylum's East Wall, 91
A Step in the Dance, 94
Triangle, 95
Passing Go, 97
End of Winter in an Old Neighborhood, 98
Cliff Diver, 101
Suomo Wrestler, 102
For the World's Strongest Man, 104
"Enough to Make a Running Shark to Sigh", 107
Fisherman, 109
A Shy Phenomenologist Breaks the Ice, 111
How the Pygmy Forest Works, 112
Life Sentences, 113
Sometimes Heaven Is a Mean Machine, 116
Song of the Woman And the Butterflyman, 117
"In The North Wind of Le Pouldu", 120
7 For a Magician, 122

I am like a room with innumerable fantastic mirrors
that distort by false reflections one single pre-existing reality
which is not there in any of them
and is there in them all.

—Fernando Pessoa—

The purpose of poetry is to remind us
how difficult it is to remain just one person,
for our house is open, there are no keys in the doors,
and invisible guests come in and out at will.

—Czeslaw Milosz—

for old Ben Fuljamin

1. COOT

MEETING COOT

Nope, not hardly local.
                        Buggywhip
in a world of powerbrakes,
that's me. Unplucked old coot
in a world of sitting ducks
and pumped-up turkeys. Me,
I'm crazy. Crazy like that loon
who spends the livelong night
trying to decide which moon
to court— the far one in the air
or the nearer one in water—
so it clammers back and forth
and back and forth it yodels
while the brightmouthed fox
stands baffled on the shore.

Nope, not these parts.

COOT'S USES FOR HIS SHIRTS

My clothes come from my needle,
some, and some from the Good Will.
I'd rather have a shirt
after it's had the smell
of factory washed out, some life
worn in.
        My own manufacture—
as you see, it ain't fancy.
Trousers loose enough
to squat down in without no rip
to scare the creatures off
I squat to visit with.
And look: This shirt's so cheap
no man'd need to think twice
to tear it for a tourniquet
or wipe off his face on it.
Why this here shirt of mine's so full
a man could hoist it for a sail
if he had a wind with him.
If he had a mind to, I should say.
There's always wind
to find a man who's stranded,
and knows it, and knows what
other uses things are for.

HOW COOT GOT HIS START, HE SAYS

I was a young man once—
set out for gold
like steelhead head to sea
or fleas make for a sleeping dog.
Worked two years in dry goods,
staked myself to a mule
and all the vittles we could tote.

Didn't have no map neither,
except the one the Lord made
and set out there
for any fool like me
to light out into.
And I lit.

HOW WORDS TASTE AND WHAT FOOD MEANS

You listen to most people talk.
You try to taste their words:
Storebought. All dried out,
or froze up like them foods
plastered with lists of poisons.
Anything that ain't natural
is poison. Ask a coyote. Tasteless
stuff a packrat wouldn't touch,
cramful of all them cancers
of the spirit and the flesh.
And then you start to rot,
and what?— They try to sell
you paint to make what smells
so bad look right.

COOT TELLS IT LIKE IT NEVER WAS

A desert in late August
must be a holy place.
Before the first sunset
I seen a miracle:
The eggs I brought
was all hardboiled
in mulesweat.
          By fall
we was holed up
in the Bloody Christ Mountains.
By Christmas I was eating bear
and looking at the mule
with a new eye. Until
he disappeared one night.
Ate him anyhow, turns out,
by eating me a grizzly
had four shod hooves
still kicking in his gut!

COOT'S LONELINESS, COOT'S GOLD

Come spring and I hit
on various things— loneliness
and gold among them. Gold
enough to keep fire
burning in me. Loneliness
enough to dull the shine.
I dreamed like anyone how one day
I'd come into a town
with ore as rich and bright
as in my dreams, rich enough
to strike the townsfolk dumb
and shut up those loud looks
I had to pass through
when I came to town.

Well, there *was* one
who looked on me so different
that I married her. Or
tried to.
      Like trying
to lassoe a cloud it was—
both of us being clouds,
no rope in sight. So,
past the first three kids
it coudn't last. Some
new wind blew.
She stayed her way,
I went mine.

"LIKE GOING HOME"

And this time getting
back amongst the mountains
was like going home.
Sitting by a stream
watching my line
was how I shopped.
Listening to coyotes
was my radio.
        I could read
the weather by the moon
and learn more
from a scraped stone
or bird chatter
than all that gossip
neighbors like to dote on.

My cabin was no castle,
but just mine.
And it was mine
because my hands knew
every stump
on every slope I drug
them logs down off of.
Not because of paper.
I didn't have no paper.
What I had was distance
on all that, for a time.

COOT TAKES A LOOK AT *COSMOPOLITAN*

Look here now, at this magazine:

>*A Blush So Real No One Will Know
>It's Not Your Own...*

Me, if I was to see a lady
stand there glowing
like the moon all night,
I'd suspect consumption first off.
And bad conscience, second.

Or this:

>*What To Tell Your Husband
>If You Put On Weight—
>While Having An Affair*

Whatever it is they tell her
she should say, she'd need
to learn to pronounce it in shotgun
if she was mine, cause
that's what she'd be talking
into the ears of.

HOW COOT CAME TO SPEAK BEAR

How many winters
come and gone up there
you'd have to read yourself
from off my walls,
if they still stand.
I lost interest in counts
after awhile.
          What I did
those years up there,
mostly I've forgot. I wonder
if there's ever rivers learn
to know their banks and beds?
But I do know I looked out
over valleys like a hawk looks
—eyes on fire, heart at peace,
the belly in me lean as a pinecone.

What else I did
was look a lot in water,
watch how fire is,
learn something about wind
from how I saw a bear sniff
out my coming one day
on a cliff: Two greased friends
at high noon in late August
couldn't have passed
there on the ledge
where me and that bear
did pass, neither of us
willing to retreat.
We spoke first is how
we knew we could.

To know what we had said,

you'd have to been
there, too. And spoken bear.

COOT AND THE QUIET

Most of my adventures
was of the quiet sort.
Like noticing one night
how my old cedar dipper
was as full of stars
as water. Then I drank.

A man inside four walls
all his natural life
cannot drink stars.
Even the full moon
can't touch his sleep
with dreams the likes
of which only a creature
knows, a creature touched
with what it is that lights up a man's skull
like fire lights up a cave.

COOT AND THE GOLDEN ARCHES

Fast food, fast cars, fast money
— it's all fast talk.

                    Now, take ideas.
They're just like grub.
Until they reach your blood
they ain't digested proper.
The gent who'd never be caught dead talking
with Egg McMuffin in his mouth,
he'll talk a snow goose south in June
with notions he's still chewing on.

It takes a mite of time
before the cut-throat trout rocks
back on his haunches
roaring like a bear with fishy breath.

"DON'T MATTER TO A DOG HE WON'T REACH CHINA"

Can't teach old dogs fancy
new tricks. Can't teach
an old dog tricks at all.
He just ain't interested
in tricks.
      He'd rather
chew on bones or follow
real scents down
real holes and start to dig.
Don't matter to a dog
he won't reach China. China
ain't what he's after,
anyhow. He's only wanting
something cool to do
while the sun shines. And digging
down on in is cool enough.

COOT AND THE SPERM BANK

I'll tell you, tell you damn straight
— This whole notion of banks is sorry
as a sinner Sunday morning. I'd never
trust a man who scrubs his nails
with anything I grub for. And this business
of "donors," don't it make the whole affair
righteous as Christmas with a preacher?
Money's bad enough, but now they're
setting up a whole new generation
to be strangers. It's sad all right,
sadder than the phoney fires
they burn up iron logs with
in bars where youngsters sit
all night working up a sweat
to record music. Hot enough,
that fire, to brand a bawling calf,
but it leaves your cockles cold
and it don't fill up the air
with the right scent. A good fire,
you can read it like a book,
your eyes and ears, nose and skin,
all working at the same time.
There's a deal of history in one
and hints about the future.
                        Lord,
I'd dread to look into the eyes
of any son of mine
my Missus had withdrawn
from some Nobel genius stranger
who wouldn't even leave his name.
You got to tend a fire once you set it
or it will run amok seeking you out.

COOT AND THE BIG TIME

Well, it was skiing
finally brought me down
and who'd have thought?
Folks bought a neighbor
mountain and brought
all those strangers in
to make it right
for still more strangers,
and they came. Just a few
at first, like the first flakes
of a big one. Then a town,
the river damned up,
rammed down its own throat
to flood the valley
with lit ski slopes, stores,
stores, stores. A city,
mind, a whole blessed city
just for people passing through.

By and by they asked,
of course, for papers.
By and by
I told them
what they knew.
Not one of them
had lived a winter
drinking boiled snow.
Not one knew what
the thirst is
a star quenches.
Not one spoke bear.
Nor hardly English neither,

to judge by what them
and their piles of paper
had to say
of what was legal nowadays
and just. Them,
they just spoke Book.

COOT'S RE-ENTRY

My wife had long since
taken leave of nonsense,
died.
      Our children,
well they said *Come on*,
and by their lights
they meant it, too. But,
it wasn't long before it seemed
they were not mine,
I was not theirs.

I'm not quite sure
just where I'll go
next yet. But go I will.
I feel a shrinking in my bones
that would mean snow,
if this was a place
with seasons.
                Pasadena?
Listen, friend. Pasadena
ain't seen snow
since Jesus drove the bus.

COOT'S LODE

It's a funny thing, you know?
Prospecting a lifetime long
and finding out about
the kind of gold there is
still in the wilderness
that no man can haul out
by mule or truck or train
or spend anywhere it is
that men are spending,
to have the knowledge
of that lode by heart
and know no human tongue
to reveal it in.
         Lord,
I've come too far by now
to trust in maps for others
and grown too worn, or nearly so,
to make it by myself.

Who could I tell?

*"Once gold was
by ants
out of burrows"*
Ezra Pound

2. "THESE ARE THE CHILDREN"

"BY THEIR OWN TRUTHFUL MASTERS"

> *The following*, writes Charles Dickens, *are a few specimens of the advertisements in the public papers. It is only four years since the oldest among them appeared; and others of the same nature continue to be published every day in shoals.*
> from *AMERICAN NOTES, 1842*

Ran away, Negress Caroline. Had on a collar with one
    prong turned down.
Ran away, the negro Manuel. Much marked with irons.
Ran away, a black woman, Betsy. Had an iron bar
    on her right leg.
Ran away, the negress Fanny. Had on an iron band
    about her neck.
$100 reward, for a negro fellow, Pompey, 40 years old.
    He is branded on the left jaw.
Ran away, a negro boy about 12 years old. Had
    round his neck a chain dog-collar with
    "De Lampert" engraved on it.
Ran away, the negro Hown. Has a ring of iron on
    his left foot. Also, Grise, his wife, having a ring
    and chain on the left leg.
Ran away, a negro boy named James. Said boy was ironed
    when he left me.
Committed to jail, a man who calls his name John.
    He has a clog of iron on his right foot
    which will weigh four or five pounds.
Detained at the police jail, the negro wench Myra.
    Has several marks of LASHING, and has irons
    on her feet.
Ran away, a negro woman and two children.
    A few days before she went off, I burnt her
    with a hot iron, on the left side of her face.
    I tried to make the letter M.
Ran away, a negro man named Henry, his left eye out,

some scars from a dirk on and under his left arm
and much scarred with the whip.
Committed to jail, a negro man. Has no toes on the left foot.
Ran away, a negro woman named Rachel. Has lost
all her toes except the large one.
Ran away, Sam. He was shot a short time since
through the hand, and has several shots in his left arm
and side.
Ran away, my negro man Dennis. Said negro has been shot
in the left arm between shoulder and elbow,
which has paralyzed the left hand.
Ran away, my negro man named Simon. He has been shot
badly,
in his back and right arm.
$25 reward for my man Isaac. He has a scar on his forehead,
caused by a blow; and one on his back,
made by a shot from a pistol.
Ran away, a negro girl called Mary. Has a small scar
over her left eye, a good many teeth missing,
the letter A is branded on her cheek and forehead.
Ran away, negro Ben. Has a scar on his right hand;
his thumb and forefinger being injured by being shot
last fall. A part of the bone came out. He has also
one or two large scars on his back and hips.
Detained at the jail, a mulatto, named Tom.
Has a scar on the right cheek, and appears to have been
burned with powder on the face.
Ran away, a negro man named Ned. Three of his fingers
are drawn into the palm of his hand by a cut.
Has a scar on the back of his neck, nearly half round,
done by a knife.
Was committed to jail, a negro man. Says
his name is Josiah. His back very much scarred by the
whip;
and branded on the thigh and hips in three or four places,
thus (JM). The rim of his right ear has been
bit or cut off.

$50 reward, for my fellow Edward. He has a scar
 on the corner of his mouth, two cuts on and under
 his arm, and the letter E on his arm.
Ran away, from the plantation of James Surgette,
 the following negroes: Randall, has one ear cropped;
  Bob, has lost one eye;
  Kentucky Tom, has one jaw broken.
Ran away, Anthony. One of his ears cut off,
 and his left hand cut with an axe.
$50 reward for the negro Jim Blake. Has a piece cut out
 of each ear, and the middle finger of the left hand
 cut off to the second joint.
Ran away, the Mulatto wench Mary. Has a cut
 on the left arm, a scar on the left shoulder, and
 two upper teeth missing.
Ran away, my man Fountain. Has holes in his ears,
 a scar on the right side of his forehead, has been shot
 in the hind parts of his legs, and is marked
 on the back with the whip.
Brought to jail, John. Left ear cropt.
$250 reward for my negro man Jim. He is much marked
 with shot in his right thigh. The shot entered on the
  outside,
 half-way between the hip and knee joints.
Ran away, a black girl named Mary. Has a scar
 on her cheek, and the end of one of her toes cut off.
Taken up, a negro man. Is very much scarred
 about the face and body, and has the left ear bit off.
Ran away, my negro man, Levi. His left hand
 has been burnt, and I think the end of his forefinger
 is off.
$25 reward for my man John. The tip of his nose
 is bit off.
Ran away, Joe Dennis. Has a small notch in one of his ears.
$25 reward for the negro slave Sally. Walks
 as though crippled in the back.
Ran away, negro boy, Jack. Has a small crop out of

his left ear.
Ran away, a negro man named WASHINGTON. Has lost a part
of his middle finger, and the end of his little finger.
Ran away, a negro man, named Ivory. Has a small piece
cut out of the top of each ear.
Ran away, a negro woman named Maria. Has a scar
on one side of her cheek, by a cut. Some scars
on her back.
Ran away, a black woman, Betsy. Had an iron bar
on her right leg.
Ran away, a negro named Arthur. Has a considerable scar
across his breast and each arm, made by a knife;
loves to talk much of the goodness of God.

BURNING

I was no one
until they made me
afraid

Made me something fearful

Until they made me have
to survive them

Now I have deeply plunged
my hands
bleeding through the dark
broken windows of their streets

I've watched them
I've learned

I've seen them breaking in
to my people
breaking in to the faces of children
leaving nothing but nigger grins

Breaking in to our lives
our women
leaving us to lie
about ourselves

Leaving us ruins

With my best nigger grin
I take their curse
I take it
I give it back burning

So I have let the old bright

currency of their being
run freely through my fingers
flowing
warmer than anything
even my women can offer me

And Lord I am changing

Lord I am consumed by change
now that I have seen myself
caving in
in windows caving in
and seen myself flickering
in fragments
on the streets

Now that I have seen myself
my whole world
burning

CURSE OF A QUIET CITIZEN

They are poisoning
the air and the water
I must daily
breathe and drink

I watch my family
breathe and drink
the poisons they are
told they breathe and drink

They feed the winter streets
with salt
I feed my car and shoes
to the salt.

They ask for my son
so I give him

They block my windows
with buildings
then offer the moon
live on TV

They hide the country
behind billboards
urging me
to move to the country

They cut down the forests
surrounding the city
I have made my home
with their goods

They force me to work in their unions
then force me to strike

They raise my wages
then raise the prices

They wire that my son is dead
and wire
the money for burial
I bury him with their money

They urge me to vote
and I vote
They tax me
I give them my money

I curse them on each of these counts
and on others

They accurately record my complaints

ESTRANGEMENTS

A man and his wife are estranged.

They have a child
they love.

The child returns from a visit
with the father
carrying a sack of candy
the mother sees and takes
and throws away.

The child cries, the mother cries,
the father, if he knew,
would cry.

The father knows.
His wife has told him
of that illness, often.
How the hands chill,
the eyes glaze.

But the father loves the child
and the child loves the father.
Neither has a full knowledge of love
and there are things
to be put in love's place.

So the child cries, the mother cries,
and the father, if he knew,
would cry.

THE DEATH OF A FAMILY

The boys swinging in Sunday suits
can scarcely be distinguished
from the grey branches they seize,
rattling them to fling the pecans down.

Anxious as squirrels among the leaves
their fathers are below, gathering what falls.
The failing patriarch abhors them all,
but orders them to stay.

At twilight in that wasting house,
the women— intimidated by relief,
regret, and willful love— surround him,
his imploring eyes fervid with decay.

Above them all, below them,
moonlight and dry frozen roots spread
and clutch, contending for a world beyond
the coins and curtains of his tended sleep.

CEREMONY

Deep in the calm of a drawing room of flowers
the only hand her father holds
is dead.

      Years ago,
behind a locked and broken bathroom door,
they found a man with eyes of dull blue silk
hanging from a tie stretched thin and knotted
in his puckered throat. She felt her father's love
as, in a shock of tenderness, his hand quickened
her arm, and loosened, dropped away. She left
them kneeling, one still, one slowly
turning, head cocked, hands loosely bound
and naked in a small bright room— her father
in the slowly turning shadow of his son.

She sits apart, alone
in the alcove reserved for close relations.
Staring through the arch that frames
her mother's face and brother's
in her memory, she knows that if her father sees
he sees her framed in that same arch of flowers,
watching, heart and buttocks clenched
as at his touch.
      Among the heads before her
she sees a former suitor's dull profile,
his wife, her father's business partner
and a friend, then half a dozen friends,
a row of strangers who look up to turn away.
She knows the faces dark with memories
she cannot know, and watches each face
patterned by the shadow of its neighbor,
watches features vanish, then reappear as restlessness
shifts a wife or husband, or a stranger

turns to stare and look away.
                          *He is gone now,
he is gone, and who are you to sit prim
among roses and lilies, breathing
this sweet stench of bright dead flowers,
breathing? Now he's gone: Without him,
who are you? Breathing among roses,
half-opened and dead, breathing
among lilies and roses, who are you?*

                          he is gone now
he is gone   please now   he is gone
the grass is soft   and look   the house
is empty   we're alone now   please
                          the grass is soft
the grass is soft and
                  he is gone now
please the grass is soft your breasts
are white and
            soft with hands and
please the grass is
                  blue eyes
please
      dull blue
            please
                  Please
                          "Please!" she cries,
and sees them turn to stare. The blank profile
turns and starts to rise, a stranger, a frightened face
that says familiar words. On everyone
a neighbor's shadow falls.
                          Outside
the sun is green in summer leaves and grass.
She sees his boy, a face pressed to the glass,
as he stares from the car at their approach. They enter,
sit in silence, and watch the child run to his mother.
Passing cars flash the sun's sharp light

against their faces.
                  "Are you all right?"
he asks. She nods an answer,
takes the hand he gives,
then lets him lead her to the waiting grave.

OLDTIMERS
for Hank Felstad

I grab my sump-pump
by the hose and drop
the deadweight down
into the dark
below the deck,
take a last look
at blue sky,
then follow down
a steel ladder
welded to the slick
bilge wall. Hit
bottom ankle-deep
in sludge, then
through a dark hole
opening through darkness
drop it down again,
again.

The dead air
of the darkness chugs.
Racket of a heart
sucking up mud,
sucking and rocking.
I try breathing
through my sleeves
but give it up.
Try whistling
but the pump drowns
whistling out.
Try singing next. Then
riveters begin to work
the hull by my head.
My brittle teeth chatter
like bright rivets.

Those lucky monkeys hung
out there in sunshine,
eyes clenched in blank goggles
while the rigid mouths grin.
You blast a hull like
that all day—nothing
between you and nothing
but the plank you plant
your sweet ass on—
friend, you pay off
debts no store on earth
would recognize.
To reach me here
the natural light
would have to wind
down sixty feet,
then search.

Next level down
three Black guys
on their hands and knees
swab it up with rags.
When one rears back
to strike a match
I can see the others'
teeth blinking
in the dark. It means
they're singing. They're
old timers. They
don't have to hear
it to sing it
anymore.

THE LAST DAYS OF A RETIRING EXECUTIVE

It started with my notice three weeks back. How could I
not have been aware before of the gradual pleurisy of
spirit in their faces red-eyed and sniffling, aware
of their faces as hopelessly flat as the quarterly
reports, of the drownings in them hourly and the clutching
skythrown hands billowing like sails eyewhite with madness?
Or the low grinding of the women's bones as they crouch
to feed the orders to the salesmen at the windows
barking *Profit! Profit!* For

profit I would come into my office blind, issue orders blind,
sell blind, renting hope to numbers whose flesh wrinkles
to vinyl on the plastic of their bones. When Mary the
half-wit secretary gave birth at my feet, her blue bastard
snarled in her flowing hair, I simply ate the child
disposing of the evidence and never noticed until now
how her eyes have become tools of conception. Now when
she trains on me those globeless sockets weeping amniotic
shine I don't know what to say. I turn away

and see it's fall again. The trees outside are rich
with validated policies, the streets are made of solid
bonds, the buildings glow with immanence like structures
blown to bits caught just as the first cracks appear:
the windows fill with faces charged by the intent to speak,
inhabited by hearts just wakened in their prisons
and boneless to escape. The one

I had mistaken for the new clerk is half-Goat, his pimply brow
broken by two horns, his human brains a pudding running
through his hair. His eyes stutter like lightning as he
clatters down the stairs after the receptionist who clatters
naked just ahead of him, her split rump flashing vivid
parts, blinking like a brakelight at rush hour. His horns

are carven gold, his breast the thin deep breast of Ram
   his neck a hump of musky folds. Her flanks are trembling
                                                                           bright.
From the waist up she is Salmon now, gasping and shining.
He takes her from behind, her mute jaws clack, eyes blank
as coins. The stairwell floods with swirling darkness.
Three *baaahs* and he snorts and drowns. She glides away,
face locked in its silver grin. The office is chaos: banks
of computers yawn and chatter, the operators buzz and
glitter.

One more week of this and I am done. It's over just in time.
   I wouldn't care to say how much longer this profession of
   insurance is likely to be valid, times
   being what they are.

I GO OUT

> *I believe we may safely assume that when
> the rate of a man's inspiration drops
> below a given level, he is dead.*
> Dr. Christiaan Barnard

I go out looking for noses
   of various shapes and sensitivities,
   each to be kept in its own container,
   airless and labelled.

I go out for hands made and marred
   by their fortunes,
   broad working hands, the long
   thin hands of invalids and artists
   —these to be kept on cookie sheets.

I go out for eyes and knees,
   ears, navels, forearms and shins,
   genitals, clean-shaven cheeks,
   armpits and moustaches.

I go out night after night,
   returning by dawn, my car
   filled with bags and jars,
   plastic sacks and matchboxes,
   identified donor by donor.

Until, Lord, I am ready at last
   to make of these parts
   one whole man.

A DREAM OF SNOW
At the Zoo After a Visit to the Clinic

Trembling, as if with joy,
palsied in her shining chair,
the girl confronts the beasts that turn
and turn before each cage to stare.

Once long cages braced the legs
now brightly hidden in soft wools,
and from those early secret nights
when, innocent, she'd study how her muscles
dwindled till she slept,
she still remembers tingling tigers
creeping through her flesh in darkness,
stalking men of sticks and ice
in dreams of cold, dreams of snow.

Now the back-and-shoulder jungle parts
and brightens: A leopard's stare
blocks the bars. His urine-yellow eyes
alert, sharpened by her helplessness,
stir her with their hopeless, deadly sympathy.

YEAR OF THE MONKEY
Night with a Veteran

1.
She sleeps and he imagines her asleep
in the next room
She sleeps and with her few words
dreams out loud among warm animals
false in the terror of darkness should she wake

She sleeps easily
now that her father who was gone
is home
He cannot sleep tonight

Restlessly he stares against his hands
hears wind in trees
the stealth of wind
tries to think it coaxes grass
from ground scorched by dry snow
here where there was snow

No snow where he has been

Fire and the smell of fire

2.
Late in a bright room
all the shades drawn, door locked
careful to keep his shadow
from betraying him against the shade
he listens
hears a car rip thin strips from the wet street
hears them tear up rags for bandages
sees the strange face bending down to his face
feels the breath
the blast

dim bodies near him smouldering
the reek of sulphur
bodies still as dolls

He feels the reaching hands
touch him as he disappears

Then the noise of newspapers wrapped around a wound
a thousand wounds
crowded
into darkness weeping without shame
more than he can comprehend
as he stares at his own healing hands

He wakes again
to the nightmare
where a figure wrapped in paper
in the next bed stares
Again he watches
helpless
as characters he cannot understand
blur with a sudden strain
and the wide-eyed man is dead again

3.
Outside the branches barb with buds
The wind slips through
house after house unheard
moves from room to room
enters each sleeper, pauses
then starts across the lawns
between the houses of the neighbors sleeping
while in their dark garages
corrupting with the rust of street-salt
cars hunch like unfinished tanks

While they sleep

and wind blows endlessly across their sleep
across a continent asleep
he listens

If he drew the shade, threw the window open
shouted
some of the sleepers nearest him would stir
and whimper
dream of someone crying
Fire! Fire!

But their sleep is undisturbed
his wife's sleep is unbroken
He knows what his hands mean
their groping in the darkness
their wooden stupor when he wakes
from dreams of bodies still as dolls
and he knows he'll endure it all

4.
It's late and he is tired
He shifts
to let his shadow lapse across the shade
and waits, trembling
Nothing
no sound but the wind
his own slow breathing

The strange face bending down to his face
and he sleeps
but dreams a dream of fire
he won't remember when he wakes
nor this crying out

The child hears him, stirs
the wound reopens
The stain spreads uncontrollably

WHITEOUT

In the dim glow of their igloo, still chanting
after months of the arctic night,
the fingers of three children dart and loop
in skillful string games. Their mother wipes
sweat from her glistening body
with skins and the precious shavings
from toys their father carved.

                        A thousand yards away
in rising wind that flattens the fur back from his face,
he abandons his watch at the seals breathing hole,
crouches and begins feeling
the long way home, guided by the iced contours of drifts
he reads with seal-skin hands, drawn on by faint songs
as the brilliance disintegrates before him.

"DO YOU KNOW THE COUNTRY AROUND HERE?"
All-night cafe

My people are like
deer
more than people.
My mother's aunt told me
this
just after I was born
the first time.

She told me
she was 13 and— Do you
know the country
around here?— her
mother
was at Sacramento,
called that now,
when the white man came there
a hundred years ago
or more
and chased them,
killing all the men
and raping
women they could catch,
the old and sick
and young. The men
died once,
the women
every time. The women
lived.
      She was
13 then
and she hid under the leaves
and they came to Booneville,
they call it Booneville now,

and got away.
She didn't have to
hide in the leaves anymore then.

Our people are different.
My people are like the deer.
Nomads. They don't
settle like your people.
It was inevitable—
your people were smarter. Don't
you think
it was inevitable?
I can see it in your eyes,
the way
you are looking at me, now.

No, no it's true.

Your eyes show me.

My people are like the deer.

—Healdsburg, California—

STOPLIGHT

Goggled yellow the cyclist's face
glares at a jaundiced world.
He cocks one leg and waits,
casual in his black girdle
of road-gear and skull-like helmet.

The mirrorbright exhaust
and handlebars reflect a grotesque
metaphor of caustic
likeness: *Buildings*
squat as cars like pike
dawdle first in still
water, then dart to strike
men minnowed in chrome.
Motion is his home.

TRUCK TALKING LATE

To His Partner

Hell no it's not my
charming personality
-- old Truck can be
3/4 SOB
95% of the time,
stubborn as a mule
in a burning barn
the other half. I
can't ask no one
to listen. All
I can do
is talk and say
if you don't like it
stick it in your ear.
It's not my charm
has got me where I am.

And where am I?
        I'm nowhere,
a shorthair trucker
getting the shaft at work
from some longhair hippy.
Now I don't take no shit,
not off nobody. But I won't
stand up to you, buddy,
and argue— what the hell's
the use
to argue? Stone
on stone, that's what.

To His Wife

Now you just goddamn shutup.
You just shut up
and hear me out.
You got no evidence
not one shred
that I been carrying on
with other women. If
I been carrying on
you got no evidence, none.

To The Waitress

Me I do not know how to act.
Truck is one obnoxious SOB.
If you don't believe me
ask my daddy.

I don't think there's
anyone on this earth
more hot tempered,
more wild, more cold
to the core than me.
And no good goddamn woman
on this God's green earth
can straighten me out.
I can be good
three months, six months,
then some wildassed turn
comes on— I'm gone.
Just some wildassed turn,
I don't know.

To Himself

I wish to hell someone
had screwed my head on
different— I was born
bad blood
in a bad time getting worse.

I got the knowledge,
I got the will power,
I got the foresight.
If I want to step back
I can see it.
I get scared.
I get scared
of consequences. I take
the bit in my mouth
and it's like a sick dog
taking a belly of grass.

I never felt a day
in my life that
anybody really cared
if Truck stayed on the road
or went on over.

VOYEUR

What is it they can
always find to say, the ones
who freeze the moment
I pull up to park
or those I happen on
in theaters, late, when
darkness is the third
member of the whispering
I never can quite hear,
overhear.
         How intimate
it seems because it is not
me to whom they speak
but to each other.
Or to themselves
in each other. When
the late late movie starts
to blind us with illusions,
when the stalled engine catches
and traffic resumes or the elevator
door opens and closes so
I hear no more,
then the empty light
around me changes—
not to red or green or
that maddeningly cautionary
amber, but to the exact
silverblackness of the mirrors
where I live, able to exist
only just as long
as I am looking on.

KANSASMAN
for Jean-Claude Marchant

1.
Me, I'm ATD,
                400 bucks
a month, I'm strictly cash.
I did my time for God
and Country trashing Nam
—Now I trash the Man.

Me, I'm "Total Disability."

You understand?

2.
Just call me Kansasman.
This here is my old buddy "Red."
He has to slop these hogs
to get his bread. Now then,
just look at him.
All tidy in his uni
and all crazy in his head.
Gets off at night all wired
just like The Chair,
you know?
                Ready for action.

3.
I never punched a drunk
but once. Meaning who? Meaning
old Whizzer. Yeah, meaning the same.
Was I the lucky one that time!
He's a pro, you dig? Or was.
Now I'd of gone down hooking
bet your ass. I'd go down

punching. Me, I wouldn't let
no man put me to bed snoozing.
If he had of punched me, who knows?
I just might of gone crazy. Staircrazy—
walk right up the staircase
in that dude's chest! Remember
that Mercedes? Remember that!
Damn near tore my boot off
but I got both his headlights,
got the grill and radiator,
got the windshield
and...I got four teeth.
3 A.M. West Amsterdam.

Now that's a fact, my man.

4.
Cop came up once, says "Buddy,
empty out them pockets.
I wanna see you gotta gun."

I said, *Now listen, man.*
If I had a gun
you think I'd be through
shooting yet?

He says,"Where you from?"
       Kansas.
"Where you headed?"
       Kansas.
"And just where is this Kansas?"
       Kansas
is the goddamn center of this country.

I told him that.

WORDS FOR THE DEAD

So you misjudged us
as you stood before
our monuments our faces
believing them
as we never dared believe

You offered
what you asked for
promised us challenged
did what you could do

And now we
have answered you
and made in you
this new red mouth
Through it you have uttered
your final understanding
with us
chilling
catching fire

Now you know us
Now we have met

The charge has been made

We are astounded

Now that you are dead
we cannot do enough for you

FOR A FRIEND I'VE LOST TRACK OF
for Jack

Today at work in a factory again
and hating it, I thought of you 10 years ago
who hated nothing, but lifted weights until your muscles
hunched your back and shoulders—even your hands:
stones—, muscles that froze you
into helplessness, afraid to fight for fear
      you'd kill someone,
afraid to love for fear of having to fight,
more alone through each year of high school,
gaining your crucial strength, your
      killing distance.

And I remember seeing you the last time 3 years
      out of school
in a park where you run up to me, take my hand
into the gentle granite of your hand
and lead me to see what you've done,
to admire the spinner hubcaps you've just waxed,
the car you've customized and no one but you has been in.
I look into the hubcap and see your metallic face
—Shining and shining and shining, there isn't
      a word it can say.

IDEALIST OUT IN THE WEATHER

When he opens his book, planes in his face shift
in its studied light. His voice
               —tentative, abrupt—
unfurls like a flag declaring a new nation.
He crouches before us, a dark radiance
               reading of friends, loss, ice,
and the land where hard men labor
coaxing new crops from exhausted earth
               for a world devouring
wholly without regard for an idealist
out in the weathers of
               spirit and the sky.
His sloped shoulders will not neatly fit
the one hollow suit he has kept
               for weddings and funerals.

His is the unfashionable appearance
the rituals of attention and despair
               impose on such a man
as the posses of high style, immaculately confidant,
declare the fashions in conscience,
               the right modes for complaint.
And this one clearly is a veteran fugitive
who will not appear sober two days running,
               whose slouch is powerfully insolent,
whose words are meant
to burn like hardwood in the winter of the heart,
               whose awful hurt
is awareness of the open mouths of countless wounds
constantly charging indifference
               as moths accuse the flame.
Gasping in the noose, still he will sing,
each death a new start. Drunkenness
               is the ax that mends his broken heart.

SWANSONG

"It feels good to be famous," he gasped,
face down in the dirt.
"I could've died of old age, gut-rot
or the preacher's threats...but
it's you that done me in.
Just think, Billy the Kid!
A notch in that big gun
sure beats a nitch
in the old lady's cupboard
—I love you for what you done."

And Billy grinned
and bid farewell
to another winner.

MATRON TO POET

Mrs. X, who prides
herself on having
kept in touch
with things,

sits beneath a crown
of hair white as an
imbecile's conscience.
Encased in slick

black silk, wellfed
childless midriff
shining
like a miner's sweaty cheek,

bright-eyed and concerned
that things go well
as such things can,
she smiles politely

at the poet, says,
"All things
considered, East Lansing is

industrious." And she can grin
diamonds.

GALVESTON SEAWALL

Isn't this "Snake Island," the place where
  a. Lafitte used to hole up between raids
  b. They aren't supposed to make buildings more than three floors high
  c. The pirates stole the injuns' wives and the injuns ate the pirates
  d. A hurricane and tidal wave made for overnight integration 50 years before the Civil Rights Movement
  e. We are now and I don't see a snake or Indian or Pirate or any waves worth bothering with, just the machine gun on that grave and all these flowers

They come to the ocean
to be stopped
in time
by the wide grey lips
and the carelessly repetitious silver
smiling of the sea.

They, too,
foam at the mouth
like nude birds
dropped forever
through the air, flapping
their meaningless wings
like knives
against the fall.

Here at last is one other
who knows how it is
to have come so far, not
caring, not cared for,
and to arrive
like so many another

at the same place
in the same way
that no one notices.

They stand there,
beercans plugged
into their faces,
hair greased back
and hung carelessly down,
doing nothing,
missing nothing
from the corners of their eyes
where the sea slides in and in.

THE CAVE-IN
for the one dead

1. Foreman

Yes, the walls *were* reinforced
that fell. Last night it rained, and the boys
were helping bail down to the firm ground
under mud as we stood at the edge,
hauling bucket after bucket
from the pit. I felt it, called,
jumped back as he looked up
and disappeared....
                We couldn't dig,
no footing. It took us half an hour
to reach him. One man cried, I stared.
I'd stared if he were mine.
I never saw a body look so dead,
so much like clay, so much like what
he died in. I guess the planks
cracked overnight. But I'd have said
that hold was safe. In fact, I did.

2. Man From The Emergency Rescue Squad

Took ten minutes from the call,
fifteen more until we reached
his hand and pulled him free. Pulled
his body free. That's all there was,
and I knew that was all there'd
ever be.
        Never seen a clay
cave-in before. I hope I seen
my last. His face was hard to tell
from what it laid in till I scooped
the mud from off his nose and mouth,

then his eyes. His eyes was shut,
thank mercy, but his mouth
was all a wide scream jammed with mud.
How deep it got inside him's hard
to say, for sure. But he was dead.
Even so I tried to clean him out,
tried to clean his mouth and throat.
I had to try. Recessitator
cain't work till you do, or then.
Machine ain't made to breathe life
into clay, but this one's worked some wonders
other times— I'll tell you that.

3. *Student*

It's such an inconvenience, all
this building. I told my parents, too.
But I was at my window watching
rain fall through the twigs
and buds and new green leaves— I thought
the coldsnap killed our vine till then—,
then it happened. I heard a shout,
a plopping sound, and saw the workmen
gather by a shallow crater
where a pit had been. But they
had made such noise since spring began—
that I ignored them, mostly. Once
a boy with blond hair laughed because
I tripped and nearly fell. I dropped
my books, and let him pick them up,
but only saw him digging once again.
I don't know who he was, but he
was nice....
        At first I didn't know
a thing was wrong, imagine that!
Mostly, I ignore them.

4. *Other Man In The Pit*

Maam, I was with him when it happened.
I was with him, so I know— he couldn't
feel a thing. Believe me, I know
because they had to dig me free
and I was numb for half an hour
or more, at least that much. He didn't
feel a thing.
       We'd just been makin
jokes, maam, makin jokes and laughin
like the Lord Hisself'd smile
to see us do. The men up top
were laughin with us, laughin, workin,
haulin buckets up to drop em
back....But he was happy, maam,
he was strong and happy at the end.
It ought to count for something, bein
happy, young....*Believe me*, he didn't
feel a thing. Not a thing.

5. *Same Man, Late In The Winter*

There's times I think it's every night
since spring I had that dream— them pullin
that boy out, and leavin me.
I don't know why a man dreams
such a thing night after night. When
I told my wife, before she left me,
at first she'd listen, let me talk
and tell her how it felt. The weight
of all that clay, the tons and tons
of clay as soft as mud but heavy,
so heavy, movin deeper, deeper, full
of stones that press my back and legs
until they snap like sticks that drive

clean through my skin. And tryin
to breathe and breathin all that muck
into your face, holdin back but breathin,
breathin deeper. Deeper.... Then
she'd turn away and say to sleep.

Can you imagine sleep with dreams
like that? I'd lay awake, I'd lay
awake all night and hear her breathin,
afraid to shut my eyes and hear
the buckets fall again, or see
them pull the body from the mud
and clean the face. To shut my eyes
and watch, and recognize myself.
But please, don't turn away, *don't turn away*.

ARC WELDER OUT IN THE COUNTRY

The darkness at midnight
—moonless, 20 below—

is that black ice of
interstellar space

through which breath
falls in crystals

when my widowed neighbor
sets to work. He

crouches to battle havoc
in a crackle of flashes

that hollow out bright caves
of visibility

the eye cannot maintain
constant

against the stutter
of that star

so hot steel melts
like wax

which briefly glows
at the core

of each failed effort
to create

out of the Pennsylvania dark
a universe

the eye open at midnight
can close to

twice.

POX: A PROGNOSIS

It starts with a spot on your cheek
that festers and scabs

over. It draws the good skin
tight, then

pulls it in. It looks
like a navel

sunk in your cheek. Soon
with its feeding it pulls

your face awry. The nearest eye
shifts toward it.

This will distort your
sense of things

until one night as you sleep,
dreaming of being whole,

the spot consumes
the troublesome eye and when you awake

you see clearly
what's left of the world to see.

Next the nose, the other eye,
the corner of your lips.

This is the worst time of all:
Blind you breathe through the edge

of your mouth

and whistle as you breathe, listening

with the ear that's left
to the pitch of the whistle rise.

Your whole face
is consumed and where your face

once was,
scalp stretches to cover.

Of course you do not see.
You do not breathe or hear.

But as long as you pretend
you can,

no one will seem to care
or scream when you appear.

"TO WHOM SHALL I SPEAK AND GIVE WARNING?"

These are the women walking and walking
hopelessly the promised streets.
Gazing back at shopwindows and bloody meats
cellophaned at their fingertips,
hoarding all their stamps, receipts,
and memories of weekend trips,
these are the women walking.

These are the men, their husbands, working,
crediting their daily lives
and nightly dying. Into the deadly calm of their wives
they press the automatic seed, investing
in the anesthetic womb that craves
her startling daughter—Queen, his son—King.

We are the children born
and bearing
all the generations of desire.

3. HOW THE PYGMY FOREST WORKS

SONG OF A BLIND TRAVELLER

As a blind man negotiates
rutted backroads, marvelling,
if he maintains his balance,
at his grace, so some men
leaning upon fences on the way
will amuse themselves
with the clumsiness they see,
while others, witnessing
his grace,
will share grace with him.

"AND THEY SWAM AND THEY SWAM"
for Bruce McGrew

Well the first thing they noticed was how those minnows
   in the biggest schools got sluggish and how
   it's the sluggish ones the pickeral pick off first.

  "Interesting," they said.

Well they took an ordinary minnow, destroyed half
   its brain, stuck it back in the water: It swam,
   eccentrically, but it swam— nobody picked it off,
   it moved too much. Unpredictably.

  "Interesting," they said.

Well it jerked along and came to a large school
   of minnows, sluggish ones picked off left and right
   by pikes and pickerals. He jerked on by, they
   spotted him and did what he did, jerked
   and pulled off the most outrageous flips.

  "Hmmm," they said. "No minds of their own. Interesting...."

Well the school flitted and darted free of the big fish,
   flashing wonderfully in and out of sight: Lost
   their predators, lost the scientific observers.

  "Interesting," they said. "They're altogether
   out of sight— Even the pikes can't find them!
   But where'd they go?"

                    Interested?

THE LORD'S CIRCUS
      As Told by the Waitress at
      an All-Night Diner in West Texas

One night last year, about this time,
nothing but that busted hunk
   of neon moon out there
and nothing in here but the roaches
   in the cups and me,
there was this pack of bikers come
   roaring in off the road in their
   black leather all
hungry for a good time and figuring
   I was it.
One wore most his own teeth strung
   out like a Cheshire grin
across his bare chest and drooled
   in a fancy lace hankie
when he laughed. Beer and fries
was what they ordered but I knew
   it was trouble coming up
when Hank pulled in, them trailer
   lights on his big rig
blinking like the Lord's circus,
the rumble of that warmed-up diesel
   muttering
like lions in the dark.

Now Hank's no fool. He seen the hidden
   knives glitter
in their eyes, the steel-toe boots
   dangling from the stools
they spun around on, staring.
He just set down grinning back and
   when the drooler
took it in his head to stir up

salt in Hank's black coffee
he still grinned and there they set,
   bumper to bumper,
while that engine muttered
   like a pride of lions
in the dark outside.

And when they run him down
name by rude name, insult by insult,
he just grinned, his knuckles
   whiter than that cup
dwarfed in his hands.
They had their fun and skinned
   him out with words
and when they let him go
they howled so loud that not one
   noticed how
he backed that flashing rig of his out,
toppling the whole row of bright
   chained bikes
like chrome dominoes and crushing
   every one
before he drove off in the dark again,
lighting up the highway with his grin.

WHY THAT BLACK GIRL PICKING DELTA COTTON WILL BE A NURSE

Aint got no nurses in Bolivar County.
Aint got no doctors
aint got nothing.
You got all these babies dying
on account that Miss Corrine
dont know what she about.
Thats how my Ma died
with my baby sister.
                That morning
when the moon still shine
my Pa woke me up
told me go fetch Miss Corrine.
I aint knowed nothing about no babies
I warnt no more than eight
but all the other womens they come
they aint knowed more than me.
My Ma screaming and screaming
and them saying oh god oh my god
praying like they aint
rightly know what they about.
Old Aunt Effie come out once
say she aint never seen nothing
like the pain Ma had to take.
When Pa took off for Mound Bayou
he done clean out his head.
He took Mr. Jeffrey's truck
something Pa aint never did.
When Pa run out I run in
to look quick. Lord it was blood
ever which-a-way and Ma just staring
her eyes bout to pop.
She had done stop yelling.
She look at me and aint even knowed me.

Hear tell that doctor aint want to come none.
Hear tell my Pa done pick him up and brung him.
I reckon he'd a put Pa in the lockup
cept when he seen Ma
it cleaned all the evil outta him.
He say the baby was in wrong.
He say Ma shoulda been cut in her belly
but who knowed it? Miss Corrine aint.
Aint never admit she aint knowed either.
She still killing people and they baby.
How she gone know?

Warnt much to Pa after that.
He just begun to stare
like something in him wrong too.
He aint never forget how he aint know
to do nothing. Folks say
he die same day as Ma
just had to wait longer to get buried.

Aint got no family. Only me.
By the time I get outta school
I gone have enough to get outta here.
I reckon I can get work
in Jackson or Memphis, one.
That'll pay my way.
Aint no big city can keep me.
I gone be nursing right here
in Mound Bayou if I lives.

HERMAPHRODITE'S RITUAL FOR WALKING PAST THE NINE WINDOWS IN THE ASYLUM'S EAST WALL

1
Walking my face electric and brave
with alcools of turquoise and opal

walking my legs magic and bright
as chrome-handled umbrellas

walking my feet and knees
walking my shell-white belly

2
walking my talent for walking
through rainlight

through sealight through hairlight
and treelight

walking my talent for walking
I think every step of the way

3
What am I wasting these
fine steps on earth for?

Why am I giving such breath
to the air? Why

am I treating these myriad eyes
blank as unminted coins

4
to me? These doctors
with pedestrian tastes

love their dogs
clipped and curled

like their women.
Lord, their women!—

    5
they love Leggs
and attend Sexy Rexy

religiously on Saturday night
then flirt Sunday morning

with the holy Ghost,
gobbling down the Host

    6
like a piece of breakfast toast
—a sop for Bloody Mary

which is the hair of the dog.
They jog in pairs, in place.

They are the plastic-faced
stiff darlings of the manikin race.

    7
My face is powdered blue
as the dazzle of sky

where my eyes are opals
like twin suns shining

through the unpredictable weather
of my manic laughter

8
as I walk my talent for walking
and parade the blade of my outrage

slicing my way through the crowds
who open like pages of cheese

and point like the hands
of a compass

9
crying out like lemmings
who catch their first whiff of the sea

as they follow me
as they follow me

walking my talent for walking
away, away, away.

A STEP IN THE DANCE

Wind moves blindly
through the casual hair
of the hobo immobile
on the moving train
— this man
who does not move,
who gets where he's going.

TRIANGLE

*After a Painted Limestone Relief in the Tomb of Ti,
an architectural overseer; Saqqara, c. 2500 B.C.*

Unrelievably vigilant, Ti
in limestone stands by Ti in dust.
The flesh on his bone (four thousand, five

hundred years entombed) is gauze on crust.
To hold his spirit, the Overseer's
pose is cut in stone. A papyrus

thicket behind his figure rears
bamboo-like stalks, corrugations
roofed by cluttered birds. Spears

are raised and a river-horse flattens
its ears. Detached, a giant
Ti—poled on zigzag patterns

meaning water—observes the hunters
and a hippopotamus. The bottoms
of loaded boats skim the rumps

of huddling, scrambled beasts. Caught
in ropes, one squats improbably.
Twists its neck. Cocks its jaw.

Ti, eternal Overseer,
staff in hand, watches close
the hunters' angled spears. Exactly

parallel, they juxtapose
against the boatman's pole, and static
shafts balance. *Control.*

Broken by a jaw, the basic
river-line provides the final
plane, creates that most fixed

and eternal form: an equilateral
triangle. Permanent
amid the agitated, vital

scene where fox-like creatures menace
nesting birds above the reeds
and river-horses bawl at men

with spears, Ti the Overseer
neither supervises nor
inspires the hunt. His figure seems

aware of every thing, divorced
from each. His body dead, its
spirit haunts a world scored

on stone walls. Time could stitch
his flesh with death, but Ti
had carved this tomb to mark his spirit.

Imperturbably alert, Ti
in limestone stands by Ti in dust
watching hunters, and watched by us.

PASSING GO

Bowlegged behind her cane
on Market street
in late afternoon
she waits sure
of a streetcar
as cactus is of rain,
her patchwork satchel
vivid against the dark
wedge of her coat.

Mist curls at
her swollen ankles
like a lap dog
she ignores.

As the racket pauses
she hauls herself aboard,
lurches
when it starts.

*Hey lady
you didn't pay!*

She halts, spins round,
points the cane. *You men,
you're all alike—
All you want to do is fuck!*

She slips in a seat,
winks at the lady
stiffened beside her.

Whispers in her ear,
*Works every time now
don't it, dear?*

THE END OF WINTER IN AN OLD NEIGHBORHOOD
for Sena

1.
Today is not quite spring
but now the Marchlit windows
widen,
       show the screen
of thin dry twigs that flinch
as sparrows hop.

   Cracking buds
perch
like beetles split
         for flight:
             gables jut,
                 bay windows
                 belly out against the wind.

2.
Today from Minnesota came a letter
from grandmother:

    Bright storms raged around us
but they missed us and we have
                a lovely Sunday morning
nice and cool
        though saddened by the stroke a patient had
Last night she lost her voice and cannot move
her eyes
     My boy you'd see my second childhood
if you could see me now   I crawl along in bed
quite on my own
           and in my infant fashion am quite free
   I feel
so free

      after these months stiffened in
traction and ridiculous in casts
We even have some fun
      The wind changes direction
often so the nurses run   opening and closing
windows   asking how we feel   too warm   too cool
                                                                 Too late
to write much more now
I must nap

      And now we've had our evening meal
One hears the cart that clatters like so many bones
and pauses
      and the opening and closing
of the doors to all the rooms as it passes   stops in silence
starts moving room by room along the hall
                                    At the end
              it waits for us
to finish
      then the clatter once again
of glass on hard white steel

      They say my bones are hardening again
Like sponge they were   So soft I couldn't stand
                                    They wouldn't
hold my body up   I weigh just ninety-five now like I did when
I was twenty and all day long
                          I wear a nightie   this one or
another but they're laundered here so often that they fade
bleached without light
                And how I miss the color
      of my hair
    "Scarlet mane" your mother called it
  and your father "Burning bush"
So short now   They keep it
cut so short

It's good to be in bed
with the moonlight on the snow
Two pillows prop my head
and the snow is like a sheet that wraps the world   The room
is rather dim   The other patients sleep
and I must close
or I will wake and think this letter was a dream
and write again and say this all again
but I can feel our winter's
nearly over

3.
A green vine flares along the twigs
        steady on its amber claws
                and as the branches heave
        the hooktips catch:
            it rides.
                The seasons
              tremble everywhere.

CLIFF DIVER

Consider the diver,
his careful fall
through fear
toward the thrill
of water glittering
among rocks. Death
is for the hesitant
who stumble.
                The one
most alive
graces that fall
with consciousness
and skill. He
wings his fears,
learns from them
on the long way down
— hawkheart soaring
in the bald body of man!

SUOMO WRESTLER

Barrelled in muscle,
cat-eyed, huge,
charged with the calm
central to a storm,
he lives a ritual feast
of gorgeous energies.

All that he has he shares
with the silent presence
who validates each meal
in the void of famine,
generates with each muscle
the vision of his own
fly-brightened bones,
appointing his smile
with signifying edge
of a pride quick to kill
gestures of vanity.

Aware of his body
like a garden hung
on racks of bone,
whose veins are vines
that redden through
the beating lungs
and brain that blossom
from the spine, aware
of the closed
circuitry of blood,
the warrior feasts
on knowing, knows and lives.
His lungs inspire
and translate into power
each fatal breath of air.

At war with time
his will wins, hour by hour,
until the years win
from his body
such an instant grace
that eyes able to see
him move see through
the trance of time,
as through a dream,
one man awake.

FOR THE WORLD'S STRONGEST MAN

> *Vasili Alexeev, Olympic Champion weight-lifter,*
> *lives in a rural mining region of the U.S.S.R.*
> *where he trains, enjoys reading Jack London,*
> *and pursues his interest in hydroponic gardening;*
> *he has developed hybrids of the rose and tomato*
> *which are named after him.*

1.
A mist fine as the hair of infants
rises from the grasses,
surrounds your town like a dream
round the head of a great sleeper.

But you, Vasili Alexeev, you do not sleep yet,
you, family man private as a bear,
whose deep breast gives deep laughter
among your neighbors, the shopkeepers and miners.
How tenderly your hands, ominous as cave-ins,
tuck in your children and your wife tonight.

You do not sleep. You see beyond your window
a scar of cloud tucked under the moon's eye.

Your hydroponic heart is afloat in your life's blood.

2.
What a man would grow must flourish first in his heart.

Beside your home whose lights, one by one, go out,
glows another house, translucent and frail,
whose light burns constant through the coldest Russian
                                                    dark.
Here you house members of your family

             from another kingdom—
the roses and tomatoes bearing your name,
both red as the blood feeding the broad leaves of your
                                                    muscle.

The rose opens from its center outward as a hand
          opens to expose an offering,
but the other, should it open, spoils its gift, and so
          turns inward like a fist,
swells into the edible muscle of tomato.

As one nourishes love
the other feeds the lovers,
their eventual sons and daughters.

So here are the rose of the eye and the rose of the belly,
the rose of persons and the People's rose.

In the waters of your floating gardens both prosper and
                                                    grow.
3.
There is the deep night of the earth
     into which your townsmen pass
          in shifts, passing the grazing

cattle that stand among the slag heaps
     underneath the claw of the moon
          where grasses silver in the mist,

\ and there is the deep night /
     neither time nor place describes
          when you put aside your book

of tales (*To Build A Fire?*
     Sea Wolf?) and, isolate
          as a stone floating in darkness,

you sit awhile perfectly still,
 hearing your house's soft breathing
  before you gird your belly, bind your wrists.

"ENOUGH TO MAKE A RUNNING SHARK TO SIGH"

> *Next come fairmaids*
> *Bra thusty jaades*
> *As maade our oozles dry*
> *An ling an haake*
> *Enough to make*
> *A raunin' shark to sigh*
>   from "The Ballad Of Tom Bawcock's Eve"

In Mousehole, on Tom Bawcock's Eve,
tourists come from miles to drink

in both local pubs, loudly singing
the wrong songs. A stranger

in search of friendly strangers,
I walk from one crowded bar

to the other— drinkers everywhere
tonight are tight as the

seven sorts of fish
crammed into Tom's Starry Gazy Pie—

and round the harbour,
the oldest in Cornwall,

I'm startled by one fisherman.
stout as a mast, dark as a post,

who will not sit
in his haunts tonight. He steps

back into the alley, black eyes fast
on the booming seawall

where storm waves rear
like pale familiars

vast as monsters, luminous
in the Christmas lights.

They crash against handfitted stones
the tourists in leather coats shun.

The fisherman stands in attendance,
cold, sober, and patient.

FISHERMAN

A woman comes
to watch her lover pull nets from the sea.

His back bulges against the tug of waves
contenting her a moment while his body,
black against the sun,
is swollen with such power
the slow dull sea around him trembles light.

She drops to her knees
and waits with sealight blowing in her hair
and with her skirt
she shades what she has brought.

Noon.

He sees her, shrugs the stonegleam of his shoulder,
and drags the living weight up onto land.
Each wave tries to drag it back.

He joins her in dry grass beyond the sand.

Wine from a bottle tall and cool
in its wrapping of wet rags. A loaf,
a wedge of cheese, an apple and a knife.

While sunlight plays on dying fish
in thrashes of brilliance,
he chews and sees her eyes darken for him
and he is glad and laughs.

They are young.
Neither seems to notice
the distant net

flashing,
the frantic sound of a thousand fingers snapping.

A pale gull slowly wheels a relic circle,
then is gone.

A SHY PHENOMENOLOGIST BREAKS THE ICE

Where there was nothing
but your silence waiting

now there is a green skull
jeweled by green eyes

breaking the reflection
of cloud on a pond.

A fly darts down, disappears,
the face submerges.

Cloudlight heals the water
with its stillness

as our faces reappear
upon that surface, gazing

deeply into themselves
in search of the argueable frog.

And things are as they should be.
The cheek-to-cheek. The mystery.

HOW THE PYGMY FOREST WORKS
Fragment of a Conversation

We were lost there
in the pygmy forest
calling for help
and nobody heard us.
Finally the only way out
was on our hands and knees
the stuff was growing so thick
and that's how we got out
was on our hands and knees.

LIFE SENTENCES

Existentialist

I'm the absurd chameleon, trying
to match the colors of the fire
    instead of leaping out.

Stoic

The madder I get the calmer I become
until I am a stone
    no one can throw.

Nun Viewing A Rainbow

Now is the perfect time
for the laying aside of old
    habits of black and white!

Apocalyptic Pessimist

Trees of the earth uproot themselves,
crying out dead fruit
    and the bones of birds.

Narcissist

What's a nice guy
like me doing
    in a face like this?

Politician

There's more to these things,
you know, than
    meets the press.

Master Teacher

Imagine
trying to explain air
    to a lung.

Jester

Who knows
what evil larks
    in the hurts of men?

Cynic

I chew more
than I swallow
    with my bite.

✓ *Epicurean Idealist*

I am all appetite, a net
flung to catch fish
    that catches stars!

Old Prospector

All gold is fool's gold
—*If you're so smart
    how come you're rich?*

√ *Mystic*

Rain speaks to the grass.
I overhear it
    and my ears get wet.

Author

The oyster's view of the pearl?
— It crowds him
    in his shell.

SOMETIMES HEAVEN IS A MEAN MACHINE
for Wayne Sloan

It is like riding Death and not dying.

It shudders, snarls and roars like an iron lion,
it shines like the chromed bones of a bull.

At night its single headlight
rakes across the highway like the lowered horn
        of a charging unicorn.

It looks like Death waiting for a taker.

You take it, you ride.

All day, all night for years
while the bright arcs of your breath flex
        into curves repeating earthshapes,
        you ride, the road informing you.

You ride
your own death and you do not die.

It shines and you ride its shining.

SONG OF THE WOMAN AND THE BUTTERFLYMAN
for Shoshanna

    Here the woman
   walked over the earth
among the nights and days
beautiful clothes upon her skin
beautiful skin upon her bones
    and from the center of her bones
   had the child sprung
      whom she carried with her
        over the earth

    Here the woman
   walked over the earth
and the grasses bloomed
underfoot behind her
and rivers ran shining
   with quick light
    wakened by her grace
      and the child was happy
       where she walked

    Here the woman
   walked over the earth
and entering a valley
she saw the butterfly
rising and falling
   in flowering grasses
    and skimming the river
      its beauty disturbing her
       where she walked

    Here the woman
   walking the valley
followed the butterfly

followed faster   lay
the child down in shade
  to follow the butterfly
    over the long green grasses
      across the river
        where she ran

    Here the woman
  following and running
now swift as a doe
removed her clothings
one by one   moving away
  as they fell sinking
  into the shaken grasses
    clouds of pollen golden
      where she ran

    Here the woman
  running through the valley
found the butterfly
waiting   found it vivid
and it was a warrior now
  who found the dark center
  of her bones empty
    and filled it with his shining
      where she lay

    Where she lay
  she rose still in his arms
as he turned saying *Hold*
here as we go— his hand
showing hers the place—
  or your spirit will be lost
  Now the woman was happy
    and did as she pleased
      while they flew

    While they flew
  she held as he had shown
and she was not ashamed
naked to the eyes of the sky
and the sun looked and saw
    and moon and stars looked and saw
    and a day passed
      and a night passed
      and she held

    Woman of earth held
  and she was not ashamed
to be available to the grasses
and entries of the water
and approaches of the air
    then she saw all around her
    everywhere   everywhere
      the wheel of the butterflies
      and she fell

    And she fell
  through a valley of the sky
whose floor was the flow
endlessly of butterflies
turning and returning
    opening her eyes to the shining
    that opens forever
      around her and opens her
      and *opens*   *opens*

"IN THE NORTH WIND OF LE POULDU"
Gaughin Writing Letters

1. 1889

I love Brittany!

Here I find
a wild
primitive quality. When
my wooden shoes
clatter
on the granite
I hear
that muted, dull and powerful
sound
I look for in painting.

2. 1889

I take my old body
for a stroll
in the north wind of Le Pouldu....

Of all my efforts this year
there remains only
the roar of Paris which discourages me
here to the point
I no longer
dare paint.
       The soul, however,
is absent and looks sadly
at the
gaping holes before its eyes.

Let critics take a careful look

at my latest work, if
they have the heart
for such things. They will see
what resigned suffering is.
        Is
a human cry
nothing?

3. 1890

May the day come— and soon—
when I escape
to that island wilderness
    in the South Seas
where I can live
in art, ecstacy, and calm.

Far from the European money struggle,
surrounded by a new family,
there on Tahiti
    in those calm tropical nights
where I can hear my heart murmur
in amorous harmony

with the beings mysterious around me,
free at last,
with no concerns
    about money money money,
finally I shall be
able to love, sing, and die.

7 FOR A MAGICIAN
for Ray Rice

1.
Out of his black hat
he draws
rabbit after rabbit

and out
of the clear air
breath after breath.

2.
It takes him years
to learn
perfectly the poise
with which to reach
into his own sleeve,
withdrawing
the blaze of silk
it takes a generation
of mulberry leaves
and worms to spin
and the fingers
of strangers
to weave.

*For the magician
about to astound
his audience.*

*For the lady
about to betray
her lover.*

*For the matador
into whose unborn wounds
first the horns
and scarlet scarf
then the faithful worm
must pass.*

Applause.

He bows.

Applause.

*She cries out
to the dark.*

Applause.

*His eyes widen
as the horn sinks in
and in.*

3.
Who brushes
the magician's favorite hat?

The rabbit and the dove.

While he tends
to the hutch and scattered nest.

4.
His best makeup
is in our minds,
the hunger
of old locks,
rusted and lost,
to be opened.

Even skepticism
is a prayer
to him,
for whom fire obeys
the moon,
for whom\water burns./

Imagine
the key of ice
designed to enter stone,
the lock made of mercury
which is its own pure key.

And look
into the clarified eyes
of just this one
who performs dreams,
who never sleeps.

5.
He brushes his teeth,
blows his nose,
eats with his mouth,
has but one suit of clothes.

He is very much like us,
it would seem,
to us.

6.
After each performance
he disappears.

Outside the stars brighten,
inside
the lights go on.

On the other side of the earth
it is morning
where he shares breakfast
with the chimpanzee,
who asks if it all went well.

They laugh as they eat.

7.
The last achievement
of an ultimate magician
is the proper
care and treatment
of all beings
filling the vast emptiness
of that hat
with which he lives.

A NOTE ON THE AUTHOR

Born in 1941, William Pitt Root spent early childhood near the Gulf coast of Florida. Since then Root has divided his time between the Pacific coast and the Sonora desert, regions he has left often to serve as writer in residence at colleges and universities throughout the country. Root also works with Poetry in the School programs, including periods on the Navajo, Hopi, Crow, Northern Cheyenne and Wind River Reservations. Root has lived in Cornwall, England, and travelled among the northern Mediterranean countries.

Root's work, poetry and, recently, short fiction, appears widely in the United States and in England, Canada, Japan, Sweden, Yugoslavia, Scotland, and Afghanistan as well; it has been translated into Russian for broadcast over Radio Free Europe. Several collections have appeared from small and major presses. Root's awards include a Wallace Stegner Writing Fellowship at Stanford University, grants from the Rockefeller and Guggenheim Foundations and the National Endowment for the Arts. During 1978-79, Root was a fellow of the United States/United Kingdom Exchange Artist program.